The Library of the Five Senses & the Sixth Sense™

Taste

Sue Hurwitz

The Rosen Publishing Group's
PowerKids Press™
New York

Published in 1997 by The Rosen Publishing Group, Inc.
29 East 21st Street, New York, NY 10010

First Edition

Book Design: Kim Sonsky

Photo Credits: Cover and all photo illustrations by Seth Dinnerman.

Hurwitz, Sue, 1934–
    Taste / by Sue Hurwitz.
        p.   cm. — (Library of the five senses & the sixth sense)
    Includes index.
    Summary: Discusses the sense of taste, including how the taste buds work.
    ISBN 0-8239-5052-2
    1. Taste—Juvenile literature. [1. Taste. 2. Senses and sensation.]
    I. Title. II. Series: Hurwitz, Sue, 1934– Library of the five senses (plus the sixth sense)
QP456.H87 1997
612.8'7—dc21
                                                                96-29959
                                                                    CIP
                                                                    AC

Manufactured in the United States of America

CONTENTS

Margot

Margot looked at the food at her brother's birthday party. She saw salty potato chips and crispy crackers with smooth, creamy peanut butter on them. She saw sweet, gooey chocolate chip cookies. She also saw her brother eating a Popsicle. Margot decided she wanted one too.

She knew the Popsicle would feel cold and slippery in her mouth. Margot liked the way different foods felt and tasted when she ate them. The Popsicle tasted like cherries!

5

What Is Taste?

Taste is one of your **senses** (SEN-sez). Your senses tell you what is happening to you. Your senses also tell you about what is happening in the world around you. Your sense of taste tells you the **flavor** (FLAY-ver) of different foods and drinks. When you eat or drink something, your tongue moves the food or drink around in your mouth. The food or drink mixes with a watery liquid called **saliva** (suh-LY-vuh). This mixing tells you the flavor of what's in your mouth. It helps you taste what you eat or drink.

How Do You Taste?

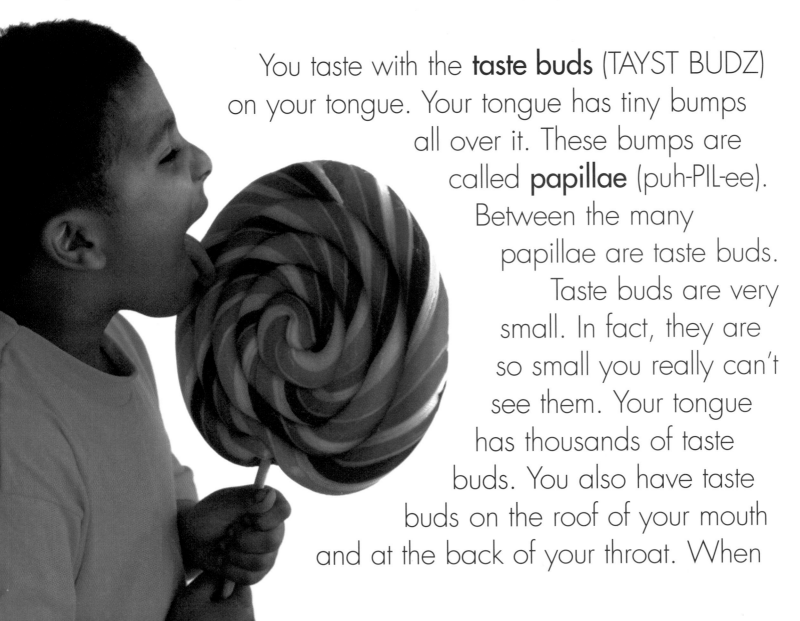

You taste with the **taste buds** (TAYST BUDZ) on your tongue. Your tongue has tiny bumps all over it. These bumps are called **papillae** (puh-PIL-ee). Between the many papillae are taste buds. Taste buds are very small. In fact, they are so small you really can't see them. Your tongue has thousands of taste buds. You also have taste buds on the roof of your mouth and at the back of your throat. When what you eat or drink reaches your taste buds, you taste what's in your mouth. This is because the taste buds send messages along **nerves** (NERVZ) in your tongue to your **brain** (BRAYN). Your brain tells you what the food you are eating tastes like.

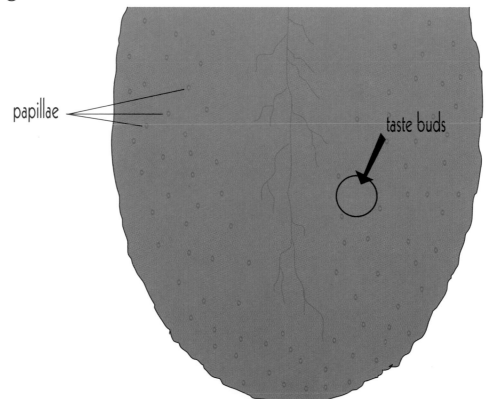

papillae

taste buds

9

Your Tongue

Your tongue is attached to the back of your mouth. It goes all the way down to the base of your throat. Papillae make your tongue look rough, but it feels soft.

Your tongue does more than help you taste. It tells you if foods or drinks are hot or cold. Your tongue moves food against your teeth, which helps you to chew your food. When you talk, you move your tongue to form different sounds.

10

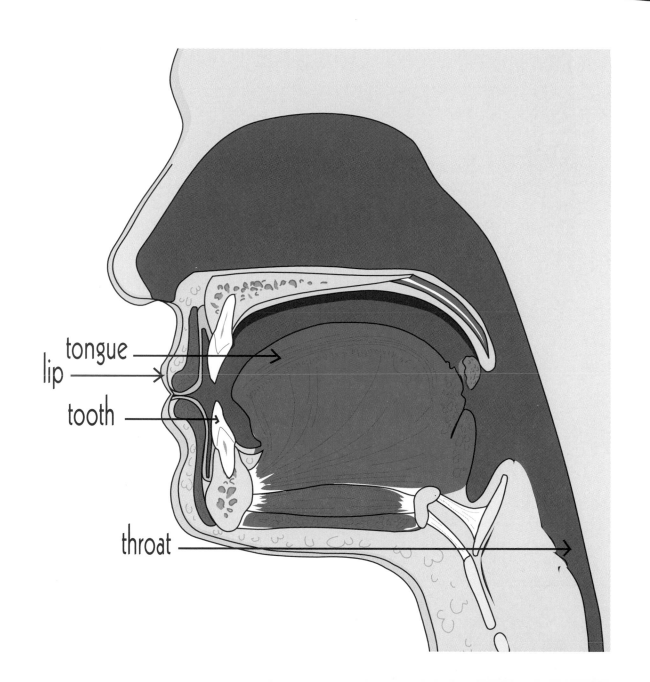

tongue

lip

tooth

throat

11

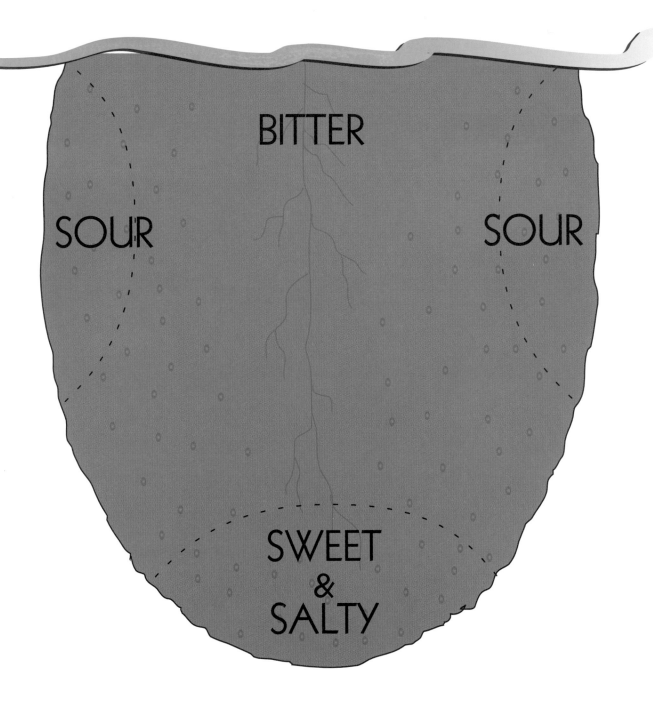

Taste and Your Tongue

Your tongue has four different kinds of taste buds. These taste buds tell you about four different tastes: sweet, salty, sour, and bitter. Other tastes are a mixture of these four flavors.

Taste buds at the tip of your tongue allow you to taste sweet and salty flavors. Taste buds at the back of your tongue allow you to taste bitter flavors. Taste buds on each side of your tongue allow you to taste sour flavors.

Tastes

Foods or drinks do not taste the same to everyone. People like different tastes. For example, most people do not like things that taste sour or bitter, such as a lemon or unsweetened tea. But some people learn to like them. A very bitter taste could make some people gag or choke. Most people like things that taste sweet, such as candy or applesauce.

15

Taste and Smelling

Your sense of taste and sense of smell work together. Your sense of taste is not very strong, but your sense of smell is. Your mouth, nose, and throat all meet at the back of your mouth.

Part of a food's flavor is its smell.

When you have a cold, your nose may be stuffed. Your sense of smell is probably not as strong as it usually is. Because of this your sense of taste may not be strong either. Your food or drink may not taste as good as they do when you can smell them well.

Taste and Your Brain

    The taste buds on your tongue send messages to your brain. Your sense of smell also sends messages about the things you're tasting to your brain. Your brain puts these messages together. Then you are able to recognize the flavors you are tasting.

    Your brain remembers tastes. When you eat something once, you will remember its flavor. When you see that food again you will

YUM, cheese!

know how it tastes before you eat it. Sorting out the many tastes that you remember may take your brain a few seconds.

Taste and Your Health

Your sense of taste helps to keep you healthy. Bitter-tasting plants are often dangerous to eat. Spoiled food usually tastes bitter or sour and could make you sick. Your sense of taste warns you not to eat food with these kinds of flavors.

You may not be able to tell if a new food tastes right. After you learn to like a new flavor you will know how it should taste. Do not swallow any foods or drinks that do not taste right!

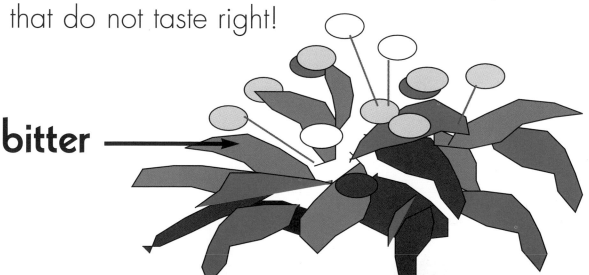

bitter

Good Taste

Keeping your mouth and tongue healthy will help you taste many new and different kinds of foods. Remember these tips:

- ᴗ Do not eat or drink anything that is very hot. You could burn your tongue and harm your taste buds for a short while.
- ᴗ Be careful not to bite your tongue when you chew.
- ᴗ Do not put sharp objects, such as pencils, into your mouth.

Keeping your mouth healthy will keep your tongue and taste buds in perfect shape!

22

Glossary

brain (BRAYN) The main nerve center in your head that controls everything you do.

flavor (FLAY-ver) How something tastes.

nerve (NERV) A bundle of rope-like cells that sends messages to your brain and other parts of your body. Nerves make up your nervous system.

papillae (puh-PIL-ee) The tiny bumps on your tongue.

saliva (suh-LY-vuh) A liquid in your mouth that helps to break up food and wash it down your throat.

senses (SEN-sez) The ways your body tells you what is happening to you and around you.

taste bud (TAYST BUD) An area on your tongue that carries messages about flavors to your brain.

Index